The New 3 Rs

of Teaching and Learning

JAMIE BRICKER

TLAC Toronto Printing & Publishing
525 University Avenue, Unit R5
Toronto, ON, M5G 2L3
Phone: 416 888 4321
www.tlac.ca

The New 3 Rs
Of Teaching and Learning
By Jamie Bricker

ISBN #: 978-1-7750664-0-8

Printed in Toronto, Ontario
Canada

Table of Contents

The Fill Up – The Bird Feeder

The traditional 3 Rs have long been considered the cornerstones of the educational experience. Ever since Sir William Curtis stated the importance of Reading, Writing, and Arithmetic almost two hundred years ago, they have forged the foundation of teaching and learning. If students could confidently decode, correctly spell, and competently manipulate numbers, they were deemed ready to effectively tackle the challenges of the outside world.

Students' minds basically served as bird feeders, where information was continually deposited until a testing situation required certain facts and figures to be extracted. Historically, the essence of teaching involved the expert in a given subject imparting his/her knowledge to someone with less expertise (Quinn, Heynoski, Thomas & Spreitzer, 2014). For far too long, the only *strategy* routinely utilized by teachers and learners alike was memory-based, and this preoccupation with recall inadvertently undermined students' opportunities for real learning.

What a student supposedly learned equated to what
a student successfully remembered.

Figure 1 – The Traditional 3 Rs: *The Fill Up*

Every student has a different feeder for each subject area.

Teacher deposits information into the feeder. Each student's feeder gradually fills.

Information is withdrawn from the sides of the feeder by the student on a per needs basis, typically during some form of assessment.

Remaining information sits in the feeder until it is eventually either retrieved by the learner, or the learner empties the remaining food at the end of the unit or term.

Regular deposits were made into each student's specific feeder for each specific subject. Teachers were constantly refilling these feeders with fresh seeds of *learning,* and students were expected to indiscriminately retain all of this incoming information until instructed by the teacher to extract specific facts and figures.

Each student had his/her own collection of feeders, as each feeder held data for distinct curriculum areas. There was very little mixing of the seeds from the various feeders, as minimal attempt was made at recognizing significant cross-curricular applications. Instruction in mathematics, geography, history, and science, for example, closely adhered to the respective curricula and were independently taught and assessed.

Various assessments throughout each unit required random bits of information to be withdrawn from the given subject's feeder. These tidbits were then used to answer questions that routinely required filling in the blank, completing some other cloze activity, or answering a multiple choice question. The exhibition of any learning was based on memorization, not mastery.

All parties were also well aware of the fact that present learning had little connection to future learning within a given subject, and virtually no connection to future learning in any other subject area. The barometer of success was simply to measure how well a given student could accurately recall the required material at the required time. Teaching was all about conveying information to the students, and learning was all about remembering these facts and figures (Olson & Katz, 2001). In addition to helping confirm how much data the student had dutifully memorized, the end of unit summative test or exam also served another important purpose: it was the trigger to empty the bird feeder of all remaining bits of information. After all, sufficient space had to be created to accommodate the next fill up.

Successful students became proficient at quickly and correctly retrieving the required test material from the mass of information stuffed into each subject's feeder, as the ability to retrieve became synonymous with the ability to achieve. This withdrawn data was then inserted into the designated place in the assessment, and this pattern of filling the educational prescription continued for decades in virtually all tests in all classes in all schools. Memorizing endless streams of isolated facts and figures led to a kind of anti-synergy, as the total long-term impact of this alleged learning was far less than the sum of these additions to short-term memory.

Figure 2 – Extracting Required Facts and Figures

Math
What *does diameter mean?*

Geography
Where *are the Andes Mountains located?*

History
Who *was the first man on the moon?*

Science
When *does water become ice?*

There was a direct correlation between the capacity of the feeder and the difficulty of the test, as the more facts that could be included on an assessment, the more studying was required. Even within a large, overflowing feeder, however, there was very little actual food for thought. Students were denied any substantive intellectual nourishment and, instead, were fed a steady diet of measly, memorizable morsels.

Being able to achieve meant being able to correctly retrieve.

Assessments based on this model were truly for the birds! They had about as much long-term accountability as weather forecasts, in terms of how much future use was expected, and demanded, of the new learning, as each unit of study was a distinct entity with a very limited shelf life. There is, in fact, no more room on the shelves of today's learners to store the endless stream of new facts and figures. As Eric Schmidt, the executive chairman of Alphabet Inc. stated several years ago, "Every two days we now create as much information as we did from the dawn of civilization up until 2003."

Trying to store this endless torrent of informational tidbits is clearly an exercise in futility. By the same token, subsequently being asked to randomly retrieve some of this information is equally pointless, as much of it will already be inaccurate and/or obsolete shortly after the completion of the summative assessment. Curriculum content clearly must provide a pathway to facilitate the learning journey, but it provides only a direction, not a final destination. Today's teaching and learning must involve far more than simply rewarding a good memory.

There will always be some memorization associated with new knowledge and skill acquisition, but to live a successful and fulfilling life in our modern world, teaching and learning must be guided by **the new 3 Rs: Richness, Relevance, and Return on Investment.** If classroom tasks don't routinely connect with all three of these critical components, then educators must honestly ask themselves, **"What *R* we teaching our students?"**

The New 3 Rs – Preview

RICHNESS

Depth and Breadth
Horizontal vs. Vertical Planes
Whys and Hows
Meaning vs. Memory
Difficulty and Complexity
Quantity vs. Quality

RELEVANCE

Learner's Lens
Teacher Intent vs. Student Impact
Food For Thought
Feedback vs. Praise
Genuine Engagement
Time On Task vs. Time Of Task

RETURN ON INVESTMENT

Genuine Problem Solving
Production vs. Reproduction
Frame It
Content vs. Context
Compound Interest
Fixed vs. Growth Mindsets

The Fulfillment – The Hour Glass

The cylindrical bird feeder model does not apply to the New 3 Rs, as under its traditional template new material simply entered the student's memory and accumulated, while awaiting isolated withdrawals dictated by testing situations. Rather than following the bird feeder model, the New 3 Rs unfolds as an Hour Glass.

Figure 3 – The New 3Rs: *The Fulfillment*

RICHNESS
Teacher generates cognitively challenging tasks that funnel their way down to the specific learner.

RELEVANCE
Learner filters the incoming data, prioritizes it, synthesizes it, and then attaches it to his/her existing schema.

RETURN ON INVESTMENT
Learner finds fulfillment in the learning task, while subsequently applying these new skills in a variety of other authentic situations.

The top chamber collects new learning from stimulating tasks **(RICHNESS)** and the narrow bottle neck allows the student to synthesize this new learning with his/her existing schema **(RELEVANCE)**. A given student's schema is a combination of his/her life experiences, skills, and personality. Finally, the large bottom chamber allows the student opportunities to meaningfully apply this new learning in other contexts **(RETURN ON INVESTMENT)**.

Figure 4 – Making It Purposeful: *Interdisciplinary Data*

Stimulating, rich tasks are interdisciplinary, as they connect across different curricula. These tasks should generate genuine interest in the learner, relate to real-life issues, and help promote active learning.

Math   Geography   History   Science

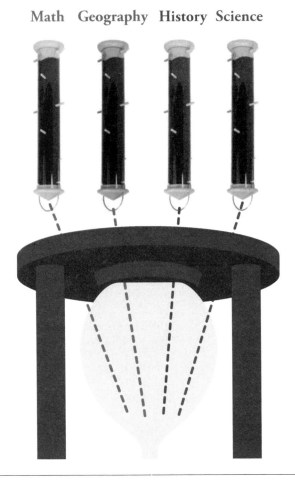

Figure 5 – Making It Personal: *Synthesis of New Input and Learner's Schema*

The relevance aspect is personalized to some degree for all students, as their schema has a significant impact on their connection to any new learning. While passing through the middle of the Hour Glass, the student's schema adheres to relevant new learning which synthesizes as it passes down to the lower chamber. Any new information generated from learning experiences that is not yet pertinent to the learner remains trapped in the filter. It is at this stage that students begin to synthesize new meaningful learning with prior related experiences. Just as the bird feeder model compartmentalizes learning, the Hour Glass model synthesizes it.

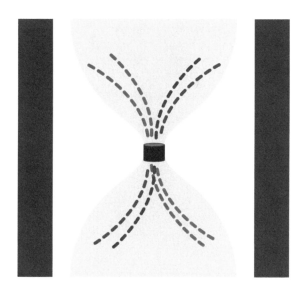

The Hour Glass synthesizes new and prior learning.

Figure 6 – Making It Practical: *Empirical Applications of Synthesized Data*

At the bottom of the Hour Glass, students then have the opportunity to apply this new learning in a variety of real-life contexts, which will help them consolidate ideas in a very meaningful way. These ongoing practical applications will serve to continually reinforce and refine the key learning and understanding. Cementing this learning legacy helps lay the foundation for a lifetime of continuous discovery, in terms of further developing both students' aptitude in a specific subject area and their attitude towards new learning in general.

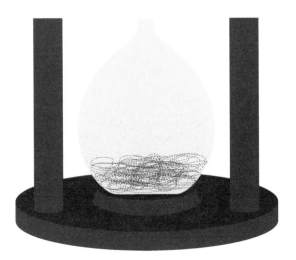

Richness

Top of the Hour Glass

Rich tasks offer different opportunities to meet the different needs of learners at different times.

Jennifer Piggott

Rich tasks are not inherently rich in isolation, but rather acquire their educational equity through meaningful applications. In other words, the key to maximizing a task's value is to explore the *HOWS* and *WHYS* of the learning opportunity, rather than simply to extract the whos, whats, wheres, and whens. Rich tasks provide students with opportunities for genuine problem solving that help develop skills that will enhance their lives far beyond the walls of the given classroom and school. In order for these tasks to yield their greatest returns, however, students must be encouraged to explore, explain, and extend new ideas and concepts. They must be emboldened to routinely challenge the status quo, and relish diverse perspectives. Finally, they must be empowered to make predictions, defend their theses, and then reflect upon the actual results at the conclusion of the task. Our students must be routinely provided with a variety of these rich learning tasks, rather than simply being given a feeder full of facts with which to solve traditional, impoverished assignments.

Tasks acquire their richness through meaningful applications.

If we continue to subject our students to an endless stream of traditional, low level tasks, we will continue to produce an ever-growing fleet of educational lawn mowers. We can all appreciate that lawn mowers serve an important role in maintaining an aesthetically pleasing world, but they never get to the root of the problem.

The immediacy of information in our modern world allows students to endlessly skim the surface of meaningful exploration, while conveniently avoiding the commitment required to dig deeper to extract richer meaning from the new learning opportunities embedded in the task. As a close teaching friend of mine has said numerous times over the years, "Modern technology allows and encourages all of us to be connected to everyone, but involved with no one." Through the educational lens, this analogy drives home the point that students can now be readily exposed to virtually any information, but how often is this information really explored?

Not only does a lawn mower only skim the surface, its sole purpose is clearly to limit growth. Watering, fertilizing, weeding, etc. are all methods to make the grass greener, but they all feed into the classic high floor–low ceiling scenario. Lawn maintenance is the height of irony, as while in theory wishing their grass to grow, in practice homeowners are passionate proponents of the fixed mindset - impose what the lawn will look like (high floor), but ignore what it could look like (low ceiling).

There is no doubt that a learner could cover a lot of material while pushing or riding the proverbial lawn mower, but they would *uncover* so much more meaning by using an aerator instead. Aeration deliberately alters a long-standing equilibrium, and literally helps breathe new life into the roots of an issue. Embedded learning opportunities are unearthed, and students are presented with a choice of exploration options. Rather than trying to superficially cover the whole yard, students will have the opportunity to uncover the particular inch that most closely aligns with their specific schema. The inch identifies what the student should be focusing on in a given subject at a given time (Katz & Dack, 2013), and addressing such needs is the essence of good teaching.

> *Exposure to new learning is not enough, as students*
> *need opportunities to explore.*

One absolutely vital aspect of exploring one's inch, is that the material has to truly matter to the learner. What matters most to anyone is material that ties in closely with the contents in his/her schema backpack, which holds a personalized lifetime of skills and experiences. The individualized schema backpack of each student is a vital instructional resource that teachers must acknowledge, respect, and, most importantly, routinely activate.

Another key aspect of rich tasks is that they offer a range of entry points that help open doors for students to ensure they can all be meaningfully involved in all lessons. Impactful teaching starts with ascertaining each learner's individual areas of strength and need, and then routinely asking questions that are inclusive, challenging, and respectful for all students. Rich tasks offer these multiple entry points and allow each student to reach his/her personal depth, while they are all being meaningfully exposed to the same overall tasks. The irony is that students must routinely explore the *depths* of a given task, in order to reach the *heights* of their learning potential.

Each of us carry around a schema backpack full of a lifetime of skills and experiences.

Routinely providing multiple entry points to lessons encourages more students to actively participate, and inspires all students to think about problems in different ways. This practice also opens many new doors for many students, but the key to opening these doors, that may well have been locked for a student's entire lifetime, clearly rests with differentiated instruction.

Differentiated tasks are designed to recognize, respect, and reward different ability levels, learning styles, and interests. Differentiating instruction means that students will be encouraged to utilize a variety of methods for both attaching meaning to new learning and for later expressing their mastery of said learning. The fundamental difference between being committed to differentiating instruction rather than simply indiscriminately filling the students' feeders is analogous to comparing checkers to chess. The impoverished game of checkers is all about equally empowered pieces following a very limited script to determine the victor, whereas the rich game of chess is predicated on recognizing and effectively utilizing the unique opportunities and limitations affixed to different pieces. A classroom routinely guided by undifferentiated instruction offers as many opportunities for individual growth and challenge as a rousing game of checkers.

Through differentiated instruction, students have the opportunity to explore tasks to varying depths depending on their schema. These choices activate their voices, help open the doors of inclusion, and provide each individual student with the keys to his/her own success. This is assuming, of course, that the assigned tasks have, in fact, the required depth.

We have all heard the tragic tales of people diving into shallow bodies of water, suddenly hitting rock bottom, and suffering permanent physical trauma. Adventurous learners can also be suddenly stopped in their tracks, if the original task lacks the necessary depth. In this case, the subsequent paralysis is obviously much less traumatic, but no less real. One of decision making's favourite clichés focuses on Paralysis *by* Analysis, which implies that overthinking a situation leads to complete inaction and then the opportunity for making that decision in a timely manner has been lost, or at least diminished, forever. In terms of problem solving, however, Paralysis *of* Analysis accurately describes situations when analysis is compelled to abruptly end simply because there is nothing meaningful left to analyze.

When learners are routinely exposed to shallow tasks, their analyses are forced to stop prematurely, as they truly have gone as far as they can go. This is a common, and very frustrating, reality encountered by many well-intended students, as the vast majority of classroom lessons don't afford opportunities for deeper learning (Hattie, 2015). When students are routinely exposed to worksheets, isolated drills, and other memory driven filler, they clearly will have precious few opportunities to tap into higher order thinking skills and actually be fulfilled.

Rich tasks allow each student to reach his/her personal depth.

Figure 7 – Prescribed Depth vs. Desired Depth

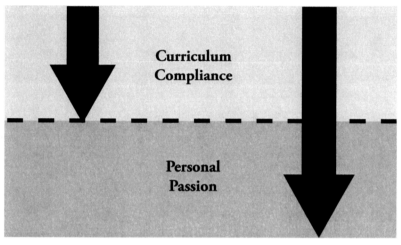

Prescribed Depth	Desired Depth
How deep the student is ultimately *allowed* to go	How deep the student is initially *motivated* to go

This marked disparity between the teacher's prescribed depth and a given student's desired depth will eventually generate frustration and resignation among even the most motivated learners. After all, routinely hitting the bottom of this pool of paralysis will, undoubtedly, diminish any student's enthusiasm to dive into other new learning. Students adapt to their environment over time, and eventually will lose the impetus to pursue unrewarded, if not openly discouraged, risk-taking. After all, children learn at a very young age not to dive into shallow water.

Paralysis of Analysis prevents deeper learning.

It is this loss of spirit for academic adventure that is truly the saddest, and most inexcusable, collateral damage of routinely imposing learning limits on students. A stark visual reminder of this regrettable reality is profoundly demonstrated by the science experiment referred to as "The Invisible Lid," in which fleas are placed in a small jar with a lid on top (Koo, 2011). Upon insertion of the lid, the fleas initially bounce off it repeatedly, as they are eager to escape. The fleas quickly adapt to this restrictive environment, however, and soon lose all motivation to push the limits and test the boundaries.

When the lid is permanently removed a few days later, the fleas remain permanently in the jar, even though they are free to leave at any time. They have clearly adapted to their new environment, become comfortable in it, and/or given up all hope of a better existence.

Routinely imposing learning limits on students robs them of their zest for future learning.

Our students also quickly determine what the teacher values and what they need to do on a daily basis in order to have a successful school year. If these expectations revolve around completing endless worksheets and other low level, compliance based tasks, that is exactly what they will do. For example, students' zest for creative writing will eventually dissipate if the assessment of their work values spelling and sentence structure far more than conveying uniquely passionate prose. By the same token, countless students have been denied the opportunity to embrace rich math concepts under the myopic rationale that until they master the computational facts (i.e. 6 x 8), they can't possibly conceptualize multi-dimensional geometry, etc. Much like the aforementioned fleas, students eventually don't even look for greater challenges, as they are content to memorize the content. The invisible lid metaphor is a vivid example of a profound self-fulfilling prophecy, as students soon learn to not even try to push the limits of their learning.

Students cannot reasonably be expected to fully commit significant time and energy to token tasks that already have arbitrarily imposed boundaries placed upon them before they even begin their work. These tasks are in fact little more than demonstrations, or actually confirmations, of previous teacher-directed *learning,* and many students rarely, if ever, get the opportunity to legitimately navigate their way across new terrain.

Successful students followed the script and became content to simply memorize the content.

Another related reality is that humans are constantly seeking the easiest resolution to a problem, and will avoid deeper thinking whenever possible (Katz & Dack, 2013). All the more reason that in order to get, and keep, their intellectual inertia moving in a positive direction, we must ensure that all learners have a bona fide opportunity to fully, and routinely, explore rich and rewarding tasks.

In terms of exploring a task, the requisite skills demanded of students are referred to as the floor, as it provides the foundation for all subsequent learning. Similarly, the ceiling represents the imposed upper limits on a given student's learning. The lower the floor, the more inclusive the activity, and the higher the ceiling, the more stimulating the activity.

Traditional, impoverished tasks offer a high floor and low ceiling, as they provide little to no room for individual variations in requisite skills and/or subsequent growth and extensions. The high floor indicates that all learners need the same basic skill set to participate in the activity, so participation is exclusive to only those students who qualify with the requisite skills. Similarly, the low ceiling means that the activity itself then offers few opportunities for subsequent growth.

This high floor-low ceiling scenario occurs far too frequently in classrooms, and it is a by-product of a deeply entrenched fixed mindset within both students and teachers (Dweck, 2006). Under this mindset, all parties expect only the *smart* kids to *get it*, while supposedly less proficient students don't, and likely never will, *get it.* Even if all students are allowed to do the assigned task, it is typically so impoverished that it will do little to enhance their future academic growth or enthusiasm. Predictably, this one size fits all learning model doesn't truly meet the needs of the vast majority of students in any class, and leads to widespread frustration. All students deserve the opportunity to be included in, and motivated by, all classroom activities.

Figure 8 – Mindsets and Inclusiveness

MINDSETS

	Exclusive	Inclusive
Growth	HIGH FLOOR & HIGH CEILING *(ENRICHMENT)*	LOW FLOOR & HIGH CEILING *(FULFILLMENT)*
Fixed	HIGH FLOOR & LOW CEILING *(FRUSTRATION)*	LOW FLOOR & LOW CEILING *(REMEDIATION)*

INCLUSIVENESS

High floor-high ceiling tasks typically provide enrichment to high achieving students, whereas low floor-low ceiling tasks focus on providing remediation to students confronting academic challenges.

To help ensure frustration free inclusion for all students in all lessons, teachers need to routinely provide tasks that have a low floor and high ceiling. Individual and collective fulfillment is attained when a classroom full of students is routinely exposed to these types of tasks. Under this scenario, all students are included in the rich task, and they then have a genuine opportunity to explore and extend learning at their appropriate level. These teachers and students are working under a growth mindset, that is all about appropriate challenges and individual growth for all (Dweck, 2006). Inclusion in these types of tasks will heighten students' confidence, competence, and curiosity, and make it far more likely that they will become actively involved in both present and future learning.

Depth and Breadth

> ## *The true delight is in the finding out, rather than in the knowing.*
>
> *Isaac Asimov*

The long-term benefit of a given task to student learning must always be measured in both vertical and horizontal planes. The vertical plane measures the depth of a given task. It addresses the evolution of key concepts across the grades, as there clearly must be a strong correlation between a task in Grade 2, for example, and related tasks in Grades 1 and 3. It is essential for this vertical cross-grade curricular alignment to be consistent throughout a student's academic journey, while appreciating that certain concepts are mandated by the curriculum to receive varying degrees of attention in a given grade.

For all assigned tasks, the long-term impact on student learning must always be measured in terms of both its depth and breadth.

Figure 9 – Depth: The Vertical Plane

The Vertical Plane – Ontario Curriculum: Canada and World Connections

Grade 3	- investigate the environmental impacts of different types of land and/or resource use
Grade 2	*- investigate the interrelationship between the natural environment and how people live*
Grade 1	- investigate the interrelationship between people and the natural features of their community

This vertical continuum highlights the shared responsibility of a series of teachers for a given student's learning.

This vertical continuum allows the Grade 2 teacher to clearly see where the student has come from and where they are going within this strand of Social Studies, in terms of this specific expectation. Far too frequently, inordinate attention is paid to students' progress during the government assessment years, and this often places unfair stress on those specific teachers. Ongoing school-wide discussion of this learning continuum within each subject area helps heighten accountability across the entire staff and creates a culture of positive peer pressure, as everyone knows what skills the incoming students should possess. Openly acknowledging this vertical continuum helps to share the responsibility for student learning among all teachers, and staff can also work collaboratively on establishing key *must master* skills that students need to be able to demonstrate at the end of the given school year.

This horizontal continuum highlights the need for teachers and students alike to make real-life connections to a given task.

The horizontal plane measures the breadth of a given task, as it addresses the application of key concepts across various curricula within a grade level. A truly rich task cannot be adequately defined within the narrow parameters of one isolated subject's curriculum, as its overall significance, and related learning opportunities, will undoubtedly encompass expectations from numerous curricula. Teachers need to encourage, and model, making connections across subjects, both in terms of task design and viable routes to solution(s). This will necessitate a paradigm shift for teachers in lesson design, instructional practice, and assessment, as one rich task can generate highly relevant data for several subject areas embedded within the task. Recognizing the potential breadth of rich tasks helps integrate teaching and learning, and results in making more real-life connections.

Figure 10 - Breadth: The Horizontal Plane

The Horizontal Plane – Cross-Curricular Connections: Blackout in Ontario

In the summer of 2003, much of the province of Ontario and numerous midwestern and northeastern states suffered a massive blackout.

Discuss the short-term and long-term impact of this unforgettable event.

Science	Math	Social Studies	Health	Language
energy issues	# of people affected	relocating people	safe food	report writing

Rich tasks transcend curriculum and should be equally applicable across several subjects within a grade level, which Douglas Reeves refers to as leverage. A truly rich task is all encompassing, and should never be simply compartmentalized into a rich math task, rich science task, etc. Rich tasks are productive, as they help students develop both a conceptual understanding of new learnings and connections among them. The productivity of the given rich task is ultimately determined by two key factors: what the teacher does with it and what the students show through it. Another key consideration for any task is its endurance, which relates to how many future applications the acquired skills will have after the completion of the given task (Reeves, 2011).

Hows and Whys

Children must be taught how to think, not what to think.
Margaret Mead

Today's students can access countless tidbits of required facts and figures on any topic in mere seconds, so wasting their time memorizing such matters is truly a trivial pursuit. Various search engines allow them instant access to a wide range of information, including dates, populations, and percentages, but the real irony of these *searches*, is that they do not require any real searching.

Searching implies depth and perseverance to the task at hand, whereas cyber searches simply provide an inventory of related information for the given topic. The bottom line is that recall type questions validate such superficial searches and do little to enhance the students' understanding of the given material. Why should learners be rewarded for spending hours memorizing tidbits of information that can be accessed in seconds and will undoubtedly be largely forgotten minutes after the summative assessment? The institutional conformity of schools has squashed the individual creativity of students for far too long!

Recall should never be considered the "be all and end all" of meaningful learning.

In order for students to have genuine opportunities to develop critical thinking skills, they must be routinely exposed to rich learning tasks. These types of tasks provide a purposeful platform from which students can begin to develop these important skills. Critical thinking must be embedded practice for everyone in a given classroom, as these skills must become expected, frequently modeled, and appropriately rewarded (Klemm, 2011). Creating this critical thinking culture clearly starts with the teacher, as it must be a case of Do As I Do, rather than simply Do As I Say.

The entire classroom culture must be one that rewards risk-taking, and encourages and values students to offer different perspectives. In this type of environment, making errors is just a natural by-product of continually stretching one's learning. Growth mindset teachers believe that they are always learning from their students, and see students' errors and misconceptions as genuine positives that inspire better teaching (Dweck, 2015).

When being wrong is seen as a weakness, it diminishes, or eliminates, students' enthusiasm to pursue new learning. We all tend to do an internal risk-reward analysis before we enter into new situations, school-based or otherwise. If we deem the perceived risks to clearly outweigh the probable rewards, we will undoubtedly decide not to engage in the proposed activity.

Risk taking prospers in classroom environments with a low floor and high ceiling, as everyone can genuinely be involved, be heard, be supported, and be valued. In order to encourage routine risk-taking for all, the assigned tasks must focus on the HOWS and WHYS. These types of questions make learners think, honour multiple interpretations, and prompt genuine, and innovative, problem solving. HOWS and WHYS are inclusive, inspirational, and infectious, as they motivate students to want to learn more.

Risk-taking prospers in classroom environments with a low floor and high ceiling.

Conversely, whos, whats, wheres, and whens should never be used as stand alone questions. These low level prompts reflect an impoverished curriculum and should only be used to provide context to support the thesis the student is defending, while addressing the HOWS and WHYS. On their own, these types of questions value isolated facts and figures that are easy to mark, but even easier to forget. The days of teflon tests must come to an end, as all meaningful assessments must have genuine sticking power. Fortunately, rich tasks create a velcro-type attachment between the learner and the learned material, as a meaningful connection is established that has some long lasting significance. Alex Trebek may enjoy sharing isolated trivia with contestants, but educators can't ever afford to place meaningful student learning in jeopardy.

Difficulty vs. Complexity

Education is not the learning of facts,
but the training of the mind to think.
Albert Einstein

Two key variables that play prominent roles in the challenge of designing rich tasks are Difficulty and Complexity. Difficulty is driven by the amount of effort required, as the greater the quantity of information to memorize, the more difficult the task. Complexity, however, is driven by the amount of thinking required, as the more cognitively challenging the task, the more complex the thinking.

I have a vivid personal example of task difficulty, which I invariably get to experience every few years. A close relative can recite all of the states in alphabetical order, while also including the capital city of each state. This in itself is quite impressive to witness, but she can then repeat this feat with one major modification: naming the states in *reverse* alphabetical order! This very impressive feat would rank highly on anyone's difficulty scale, but it is not the least bit complex.

Complex tasks require higher level thinking, such as those skills highlighted at the more advanced levels of Bloom's Taxonomy. The revised version of Bloom's has deemed creativity as its highest level, as students must be encouraged, and expected, to routinely think outside the box. These types of tasks allow, and require, students to dig deeper into the learning material, and there will typically be more than one viable answer. Being routinely exposed to rich tasks both helps, and necessitates, students develop different skills, and also provides them with some useful insights into their own learning. The expectations of any task become more complex, whenever students are required to apply, analyze, evaluate, and create, rather than simply memorize and recall new information. How can being routinely rewarded for withdrawing random minutia from feeders full of facts possibly help develop any of these skills?

Routine exposure to rich tasks develops different skills in students.

Whenever the quantity of material remembered is more highly valued than the quality of thoughts and ideas generated, then low level learning is being encouraged and reinforced. In the past, the amount of time spent studying was typically regarded as a badge of honour, as there was generally a direct correlation between time spent memorizing testable facts and the ease with which this information could be quickly recalled under the pressure and time constraint of the summative assessment.

This informational assembly line would have made Henry Ford proud for its efficiency, as the same pattern of learning repeated itself over and over again for decades. Just as Ford famously uttered, "Any customer can have a car painted any colour that he wants so long as it is black," the traditional educational assembly line has functioned within similar constraints. The word *recall* has ominous repercussions in both of these enterprises. In the automotive world, it acknowledges the need to correct a flawed product, while in the educational world, it acknowledges the basis of a flawed system.

Ford offered few variations to his product and educators have given students very few, if any, meaningful opportunities to provide input as to what they would like to specifically learn about a given concept. There obviously needs to always be a government generated curriculum for everyone to follow, but considerably more school and classroom flexibility should also be provided to help make that material come to life for the given students.

Teachers need to make a concerted effort to ensure that assigned tasks reflect the schema of their specific students whenever and wherever possible. In reality, however, a classroom full of students presents a wide range of interests and experiences, and clearly no one task is going to align with all of them. To effectively address this situation, teachers need to work with students to establish common classroom schema developed through read-a-louds, field trips, guest speakers, and any other school-based learning opportunities.

Developing a common classroom schema in no way undermines or minimizes the importance of recognizing and valuing the unique schema of individual students, but rather it helps establish a more level experiential playing field for all.

> *Lower level learning values quantity of material learned more so than its quality.*

R you routinely enriching tasks...

- *Providing significant DEPTH and BREADTH to tasks, by transcending specific grade and subject*
- *Focusing on the HOWS and WHYS in all questioning and class discussions*
- *Emphasizing COMPLEX TASKS over difficult tasks*

Relevance

Middle Of The Hour Glass

Relevance gives students a context within which they can develop into engaged, motivated and self-regulated learners.

Saga Briggs

For any learner to become fully invested in a given task, he/she must find it relevant to his/her existing schema. Every person's unique collection of experiences, skills, and personality traits is stored in a schema backpack, that we all involuntarily carry around with us each and every day. Some key components of a person's backpack become more fixed throughout their lifetime, such as one's value system and core beliefs. Much of the backpack's composition remains fluid, however, as new situations arise and existing skills and interests are constantly being reinforced, refined, or replaced.

The most significant change between the Fill Me Up Bird Feeder model of decades past and the Fulfill Me Hour Glass model of the new 3 Rs is the bottle neck in the middle of the learning cycle. This narrowing, and slowing, of the flow of facts and figures is where relevance to the learner becomes a vital part of the whole process. At this point, the learner is entitled and encouraged to filter the incoming information. These new skills and this acquired knowledge can then ultimately either be attached to his or her existing schema and passed down to the lower chamber, or be left in the filter until they become more meaningfully connected to the student during a future task. It is in this middle filter of the Hour Glass that student voice begins to truly resonate.

"Students must be seen as partners in change, rather than merely targets of change" (Hargreaves & Shirley, 2009), and a big part of this mandate includes permitting and promoting genuine student voice in planning future learning opportunities. A key aspect of this student voice has to do with the degree of autonomy the learner is given with regard to his/her learning, as each student must feel truly empowered.

Student voice resonates loudest in the middle of the Hour Glass.

During this vital passing through the middle channel, the learner begins to synthesize new information with his/her existing schema to help make new learning both purposeful and productive. Previous learning and experiences are combined with relevant aspects of the new data, and this combination is then funneled through the individual student's filter. This filtering process is critical, as it identifies and refines the key commonalities between prior and present learning, and helps set the foundation for future applications of these skills and related knowledge.

Figure 11 – The Funnel at the Top of the Hour Glass

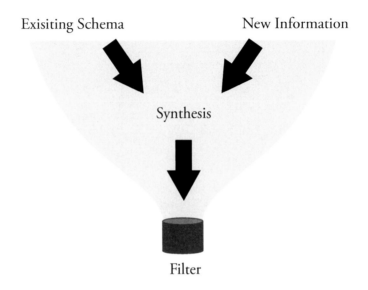

Exisiting Schema   New Information

Synthesis

Filter

A given student's yearning for future learning is typically motivated by either personal passion or perceived purpose. Passionate relevance is genuine, as the learner's schema backpack contains either positive or negative memories that he/she wishes to address. In other words, the learner has a long-established connection, or attachment, to key aspects of the task. The given task has triggered memories of either past successes that he/she would like to relive, or past failures that he/she would like to revise. Either way the learner is legitimately motivated to do well. An example of passionate relevance would be a person's resolution to get into better physical condition, so that he/she can be more active and lead a more rewarding life.

Purposeful relevance is disingenuous, and fabricated for a particular reason. Tasks that generate purposeful relevance have little or no connection to the composition of the learner's schema backpack. The learner imposes an artificial importance on material simply to better his/her chances of attaining the desired goal, whether it be higher marks, a promotion, etc. The perceived purpose could come from the learner's pride, parental expectations, or standards imposed by other adults. Learners do their best to create a contrived connection to the given task in hopes of heightening both their initial level of interest and their ultimate level of achievement. An example of purposeful relevance would be a professional athlete trying to convince himself/herself to get into better physical condition, after the coach threatens to impose heavy fines if he/she fails to do so.

Students are motivated to learn by either personal passion or perceived purpose.

It is especially important for teachers to routinely provide relevant tasks for students struggling with concepts, as these learners are desperate to make it as real as possible. The cruel irony, and inexcusable reality, is that these students typically receive by far the fewest opportunities to apply concepts in real-life situations, as they get repeatedly drilled with isolated content. The misguided rationale is that students need to master the lower level content skills before they can possibly be successful with any practical applications. Contextual applications are considered an extension, or reward, for those students who have mastered the content. Routine exposure to meaningful material needs to be a right, not a reward!

Obviously students need to acquire some proficiency with basic skills and content, but they should not have to endure prolonged isolation from contextual relevance before earning the right for meaningful applications. Relevant applications provide a great opportunity for students to both show and grow their learning. Providing different entry points allows all students to be actively involved in the same meaningful task, while acknowledging the disparities in their respective skill sets. Conversely, forcing all students to keep knocking on the same locked door undoubtedly leads to learned helplessness, which ultimately leads to long-term hopelessness.

Learner's Lens

> ## The best teachers are those who show you where to look, but don't tell you what to see.
> *Alexandra K. Trenfor*

Beauty is in the eye of the beholder, and relevance is in the lens of the learner. In all learning situations, every decision needs to recognize and respect the legitimacy of the learner's lens. By far the most important concern in assessing the relevance of any learned material is always the view of the given student.

The legitimacy of the learner's lens must always be recognized and respected.

This key message was driven home to me a few years ago. My elder son was then in his late teens and we were watching television one evening. When a commercial came on that previewed some scenes from Adam Sandler's upcoming movie, I mumbled some disparaging comments about his work. At that point, my son interjected that fortunately for Mr. Sandler, I was not his target demographic. We then got into a discussion about why media outlets routinely send middle aged adults to review movies that are intended for a teenage audience. The reviewer's lens will likely have little or nothing in common with the typical teenager's lens when it comes to their opinions of a movie, television show, book, etc. Without question, my son had an extremely valid point! During this chat, I vividly remember having an "Aha" moment, as there were clearly educational implications linked to this fundamental disconnect.

The unmistakable message to me was that prior to assigning any task, the teacher must always make a concerted effort to see the proposed work through both the collective and individual learner's lens:

- *Does this task offer the individual learner a chance to personalize his/her focus, to help activate his/her own interests, abilities, and needs?*

- *Does this task offer multiple layers of challenge, so that all learners will be meaningfully engaged?*

- *Does this task offer, encourage, and reward multiple representations of the solution?*

- *Does this task offer opportunities to deploy higher level thinking skills?*

Teachers need to always be aware that their idea of a highly engaging task for a certain age/grade of students may not necessarily hit the mark from the students' perspectives. In addition, even if the collective lens of the overall class feels quite connected to the assignment, there will inevitably be a pocket of students who feel that it has badly missed the mark. Teachers need to always consider the learner's lens, as "when you go fishing, what do you put on the hook…what you like or what the fish likes?" (Capacity Building Series, 2011).

Figure 12 – Through The Learner's Lens

The learner's lens is actually a unique series of lenses generated by the composition of the given learner's schema backpack.

Learner's Lens
(Schema Backpack)

For all of us, our perception is in fact our reality. All of our lenses have a certain degree of bias, based on our own schema, and our students are no different. Confirmation bias impacts the willingness of all of us to embrace new learning, as we naturally expect past trends to continue. Prior success in a subject triggers pleasant memories and makes it far more likely that a student will embrace new learning. Conversely, think of how many adults freely share their profound lack of competence and confidence in mathematics, which serves as a convenient cop-out to avoid new learning. Past failures and frustrations can certainly lead to work avoidance and a profound lack of risk-taking. When students' lenses don't see a clear path to success, they can either get argumentative or apathetic towards a new task. Both of these reactions serve as social defense mechanisms, as students of all ages would much prefer to be seen as "I won't" rather than "I can't."

As much as activities and assigned tasks are driven by the curriculum expectations, teachers must always be aware of any significant disconnects between the intent of the lesson and its actual impact on the students. All learners have a unique schema backpack, and in terms of both lesson planning and execution, one size definitely does not fit all. Learners require, and develop, different lenses over time, as they acquire experience and expertise, to truly "see what you mean."

Food For Thought

Feedback is the breakfast of champions.
Ken Blanchard

Under the traditional 3 Rs, students rarely had time to focus their lenses on the given material, as there was no intellectual friction to slow down the steady descent of random facts and figures dropping to the bottom of the bird feeder. In other words, incoming information was not prioritized by, or connected to, the learner, so it simply accumulated. Consequently, most assessments involved teflon test tidbits that did not stick long-term to the learner. Out of sight, out of mind, and on to the next unit of study.

Many teachers took considerable comfort in meticulously collecting the myriad of marks that were generated by these bird feeder emptying assessments. This data could be shared with students, parents, and administration throughout the school year. It's ironic that they then typically used all of these marks to determine a mean average, as what, if anything, these marks actually *mean* is open to considerable debate. This data certainly provided an accurate ranking of each student's recall and retrieval skills, but offered little in terms of addressing future learning needs. Rather than simply producing a superficially quantifiable mark, the major purpose of assessments should always be to provide valuable feedback to teachers.

Student assessments generate valuable feedback for teachers.

Feedback serves an important, and impactful, purpose, as it helps to clearly outline where they should go next in the teaching process. "The problem is that right now we see the purpose of the test as informing the student, not the teacher" (Hattie, 2009). The old adage about strength in numbers rarely, if ever, applies to the generation of quality feedback. The relative impact of any feedback is directly correlated to the quality of the assignments, not the quantity of the assessments.

There is absolutely no question that genuinely praising students for exhibiting valued character traits, such as honesty and integrity, is extremely important and teachers should continue do so on a regular basis. Similarly, when students engage in their work with enthusiasm and/or exhibit appropriate manners, these efforts should certainly be acknowledged. There must, however, always be a fundamental distinction between delivering personal praise and offering performance-based feedback. Praise is all about the person, whereas feedback needs to be all about his/her work. Well-intended clichés such as "good job" and "keep it up," for example, provide absolutely no meaningful feedback. Feedback must always be specific and practical, and leave the learner with some clear steps to follow on the road to heightened student achievement.

The potential impact of feedback is one key area in which the 3 Rs are very closely aligned: Rich tasks provide the basis for higher quality feedback, this feedback is more Relevant to the given learner as it specifically addresses his/her strengths and needs, and this feedback provides the greatest Return On Investment, as students are better equipped to generate new learning opportunities through future applications. There is a strong correlation between the challenge of the task and the power of the feedback (Hattie, 2009). Assigning students impoverished tasks is clearly going to deny them the chance to receive rich feedback.

The teacher's challenge is to structure a collaborative, supportive classroom environment in which risk-taking is the norm and feedback is frequent and specific to academic progress. Feedback closes the gap between intent and impact or, in other words, the gap between the learner's lens and the teacher's lens.

Feedback must always be clear, concise, and task specific.

Figure 13 – The Role of Feedback

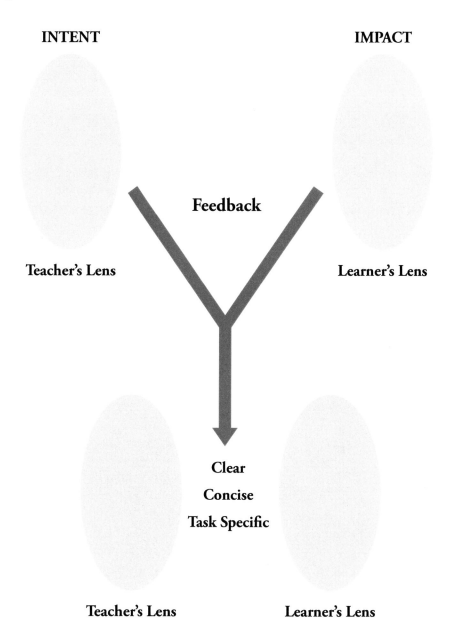

Authentic Engagement

I would rather have one day of authentic student engagement than a career handing out worksheets.
Sean Junkins

Speaking of lenses, student engagement has been viewed through the classroom management lens for way too long. Far too often, student engagement has become synonymous with student compliance, as the goal for many teachers is to have students work quietly on the assigned low level task. Authentic engagement involves far more than simply keeping students occupied by their work, as they need to feel both intellectually challenged and purposefully connected to the given task.

Authentic engagement requires both intellectual challenge and purposeful connection.

Challenge is one of the core ingredients of effective learning, but the art is making the challenge appropriate for the student. This is why relating a task to prior learning is so important. After the teacher determines an appropriate level of challenge, for a given student to get fully invested in a task he/she must find it pertinent to his/her schema. Having teachers develop a real understanding of the interests and experiences of their students is one of the key components of creating a welcoming and collaborative classroom culture. Skilled teachers frequently do gap analyses of where students are compared to where they need to be through a curriculum content lens, but they also need to always recognize and appreciate the students' perspectives. This type of ongoing analysis will help to build, and maintain, a bridge between mandated curriculum concepts and genuine student interests.

The given student's perspective on different learning activities has a direct impact on the level, and length, of his/her engagement. As such, there is a clear correlation between the type of relevance that is motivating the learner, and his/her enthusiasm and engagement for the given task. A student's level of engagement for any task will always be higher whenever it genuinely interests him/her (i.e. passionate relevance), rather than when the learner is trying to make it seem interesting simply to get a good mark (i.e. purposeful relevance). Students who succeed through purposeful relevance should be truly commended for their focus and determination, but their learning will likely have little shelf life beyond the completion of the unit. Their manufactured motivation to learn was a means to an end, and the end of the unit typically means the end of that learning.

True student engagement generates questions, discussions, agreements, disagreements, and quite often somewhat elevated voices. First and foremost, it triggers passion in the learner! They want to do the task, they want to learn, they want to know more, and they want, and deserve, the opportunity to keep working at it. In other words, the learner is truly committed to the task.

Discussions regarding student engagement undoubtedly make reference to the importance of the student's Time *On* Task. The key underlying, and seemingly quite logical, belief has been that the more engaging the task, the longer the student will persevere with it. By extension, the longer the student perseveres, the more he or she will learn. This premise clearly has some merit, but students can happily spend an inordinate amount of time on pretty petty tasks (i.e. colouring maps, filling in worksheets). The real question needs to be Time *Of* Task. In other words, how long after its completion will a given task have any significant impact on the student's subsequent learning? How much will the task matter to the student days and weeks after its completion?

Teachers must always ask themselves, what impact a given task will have on any future learning.

The typical worksheet provides the most profound distinction between Time *On* Task and Time *Of* Task. The vast majority of students routinely put forth considerable time and effort into completing the daily deluge of worksheets, by filling in the blanks and/or colouring in the pictures. Routine exposure to such cognitively limiting cloze activities will undoubtedly close active minds in our students.

Depending on the number of sections to be coloured or the number of questions to be answered, many of these worksheets typically yield a rather impressive Time *On* Task. The fact most of these sheets will be lost or placed in the classroom recycling bin within hours, if not minutes, of completion, however, reinforces their extremely low Time *Of* Task. Mindlessly filling a recycling bin at the end of each school day may well be environmentally appealing, but mindlessly filling a student's mind each day is educationally appalling!

Connecting present and future undertakings to prior learning and experiences, is one of the key components of the process involved in personalizing a task. Once these connections have been established and legitimized, then the learning is deemed purposeful and students are much more likely to stay motivated and focused.

R you routinely ensuring tasks are relevant to the learner by...

- *Acknowledging the LEGITIMACY OF THE LEARNER'S LENS*
- *Providing the learner with TIMELY AND RELEVANT FEEDBACK*
- *Triggering and maintaining AUTHENTIC STUDENT ENGAGEMENT*

Return on Investment
Bottom of the Hour Glass

A sense of fulfillment is an awareness that our talents are being unearthed and put to a positive use as we grow into the people we are capable of being.

Tom Morris

Everyone needs to see a reasonable return on their financial investments, and the same premise most definitely applies to our students. With educational investments, however, one key question involves the shelf life of the learning goals for the assigned tasks. Will a student remember and, more importantly, value the point of a given unit of study a month after the summative assessment, or will it simply be another item checked off the long list of *must dos* at school? The assigned tasks will have far more sustainable educational endurance for the learner if he/she sees legitimate links to the real world. Students will understandably be much more connected to their work if it is rightfully connected to both their present and future worlds beyond both classroom and school walls.

Student assigned work must be validated by legitimate real-world connections.

If the students aren't connected with their work, they probably won't remember it days later, and then there will clearly be little or no Return On Investment (ROI). This stage is critical in helping facilitate the ongoing creation and exploration of more rich tasks. Rich tasks have the capability to generate a significant Return On Investment, whereas impoverished, traditional tasks produce little more than simple interest. Simple interest implies that while the activity may be fun or interesting at the time for some students, it is an isolated event with little or no reasonable opportunity, or expectation, to yield any future dividends. Considering the time invested by both the learner and teacher, in addition to the ever growing costs associated with education, generating only simple interest is simply unacceptable!

Due to a combination of the large quantity of undifferentiated data and few, if any, opportunities for the student to synthesize this information, new learning is rarely meaningfully applied. Far too often we ask students to select from the bargain bin of tasks and then unreasonably expect them to generate a significant return on this investment.

Teachers can be instrumental in significantly increasing the Return On Investment that students derive from a given task. The more teachers model how to make connections and encourage students to augment their schema, the more lasting the learning investment for the given student. Rather than focusing on the short-term expectations of what to learn, focusing teaching and learning on the long-term explorations for how to learn will yield the greatest return (Katz & Dack, 2013).

Figure 14 – Generating Sustainable Return On Investment

Students' Return On Investment	Impoverished & Isolated Tasks	**Rich & Relevant Tasks**
Learning Legacy	Generate Simple Interest *"It was fun"*	**Generate Compound Interest** *"I want to learn more"*
Derived Dividends	Additions to Short-Term Memory	**Applications of Long-Term Meaning**
Teaching Focus	What To Learn	**How To Learn**
Educational Priorities	Compliance & Recitation	**Creativity & Innovation**

Following the very successful Google model based on the free development of ideas, some students across North America have in fact had the invaluable opportunity to routinely explore *how to learn.* Employees at Google are afforded up to 20% of their work day to devote to projects that are of particular interest to them. Some teachers have developed Genius Hour that similarly allows, and encourages, students to spend part of their time working on these types of projects (Heick, 2014). Students have considerable academic freedom regarding their specific hypothesis, investigative process, and presentation of findings.

What is the potential Return on Investment from Genius Hour? Much like with the Google plan itself, the greatest ROI is that it provides a forum for students to be creative and innovative. Our education system must value passionate innovation far more than programmed recitation.

Passionate innovation must be valued far more than programmed recitation.

Genuine Problem Solving

> *Problems are only opportunities in work clothes.*
> *Henry J. Kaiser*

Students deserve the opportunity to create an original production, rather than always feeling compelled to share their version of a mass reproduction. The learning goal of any task is obviously driven by the curriculum, but the chosen pathway to this destination warrants a lot of genuine student input, if the required journey is going to make any lasting impression on the travellers. It is not simply a case of plugging in the teacher's GPS and being guided to the prescribed destination. In fact, much of the key learning is derived from determining the best route, and alternate paths must be valued. The key is to value the route, while minimizing the rote, as students learn to recognize and appreciate more than one pathway to their destination. Genuine problem solving requires students to forge their own path, whereas contrived demonstrations simply provide them with a map to follow and greatly reduce the legitimacy of both the task and the subsequent learning.

Students must be encouraged to forge the route,
not simply follow the rote.

Demonstrations of a concept are erroneously presented as problem solving in many classrooms and textbooks, but with these types of *problems* the teacher simply maps out the path at the beginning of the unit and takes the students along for the ride. In mathematical or scientific pursuits, students are simply required to repeatedly insert the required numbers into the required spot in the required algorithm to derive the required answer. In many other disciplines, all students have to do is similarly adhere to a mandated template largely driven by the whats, wheres, whos, and whens, with few embedded opportunities to truly explore the HOWS and WHYS. It routinely becomes a contrived opportunity to confirm student learning of adult-driven teaching, rather than a genuine opportunity for student-driven discovery.

These alleged confirmations of learning inevitably produce student work that all looks very similar, if not identical, as all students are following the same teacher imposed script. Far too little academic freedom and far too much teacher direction combine to produce far too similar student work.

Figure 15 – Students Simply Following The Script

Too Little   **+**   **Too Much**   **=**   **Too Similar**
Task Depth   **Teacher Input**   **Student Output**

Real problem solving opportunities must present themselves in learning environments that are supportive, non-judgmental, and recognize the value in making mistakes. An invaluable part of this process is having the learner make an informed prediction of the outcome, complete the process, and then reflect on the accuracy, or lack thereof, of the prediction. Many problem solving templates understandably place a premium on concluding with a reflection stage. Focused reflections have always been a very important part of any meaningful learning, but they quickly lose their impact without predictions being made prior to beginning the given task. Without making a prediction, upon what exactly will the learner later be reflecting? There is obviously an inherent bias in any after the fact reflection for which there had not been a prediction. After all, hindsight is always 20/20. All the more reason why students should routinely utilize appropriate experiences from their schema backpacks to help them generate a viable hypothesis of what will ultimately happen prior to beginning a task, as this process is one of the foundational steps to meaningful learning.

The most profound learning generally occurs when a prediction is proven to be incorrect, as the student is then genuinely motivated to explain the gap between the expected and the experienced. Methodically reviewing all of the decisions made during the completion of a rich and relevant task can facilitate the teacher effectively addressing some key student misconceptions, before they become more permanently ingrained and all the more difficult to correct. All of this has to be done in a supportive classroom environment full of committed learners, however, as when it comes to truly addressing misconceptions, slow and steady wins the race. As Carol Dweck states, "speed and perfection are the enemy of difficult learning" (Dweck, 2006).

Frame It

> ## *For me context is the key – from that comes the understanding of everything.*
> *Kenneth Noland*

Teaching is a combination of science (the picture frame) and art (the canvas). The curriculum provides the dimensions of the frame, within which both teaching and learning will, and must, occur. In other words, the context for the particular learning is established, or rather imposed. Within these boundaries, however, students need, and deserve, the academic freedom to create their own productions. After all, if all students are doing the same undifferentiated work at the same time, then in essence each student is basically doing nothing more than painting by numbers.

Students all doing the same thing at the same time is little more than painting by numbers.

Effective teachers provide each student with a brush, to help them consolidate key skills within the context of this picture frame. The art is to connect students' existing schema with the relevant content skills. A blank canvas presents infinite possibilities, and within the dimensions of the frame each student deserves the opportunity to explore his/her personal possibilities to the fullest. The most impactful learning occurs when the contributions of different learners blend together on the canvas and create a new tertiary colour. This colour signifies the powerful synergy of collaborative, creative thought.

It is far too easy, and highly ineffective, for teachers to seemingly encourage student exploration of a concept, but then conclude the lesson by using their proverbial roller to alter, override, or simply ignore some or all student input. Enthusiasm for engaging in similar tasks in the future will certainly be significantly reduced if students feel their ideas have been given the brush off.

As previously discussed, for students to contribute on the canvas, they will need to demonstrate a solid understanding of basic, foundational skills, and concepts (Hattie, 2015). Without these requisite content skills, diving into contextual applications will lead to failure and frustration, as well as likely magnify existing misconceptions and/or create new ones. The key involves acknowledging the need for balance, as focusing entirely on context-free content until key skills are mastered is equally counterproductive, as it will simply turn them off future learning. Many students will never master all of the underlying content-based skills, but can still demonstrate very clear understanding of the broader contextual applications.

Many students can correctly apply concepts without having mastered all content.

It is highly questionable in any area of endeavour if practice does in fact make perfect. What is undeniable, however, is that for far too many students, practice *is permanent.* Any student can only practice isolated content-based drills for so long, without having the opportunity to play the game. Golfers will never reach their potential if they only hit balls at a driving range, musicians will never reach their potential if they only play scales and chords, and students will never reach their potential if they only practice isolated skills. After all, besides heightened interest, playing the game is the only way for students to really learn how things all fit together (Perkins, 2010). Routinely exposing students to legitimate game situations is also the best way for them to develop legitimate problem solving skills. Many classroom environments inadvertently increase the problem solving skills' gap among students, as more proficient learners typically receive far more opportunities to play the game, while those struggling with concepts must endure endless practice of isolated skills. If students are struggling with the content, and never get to experience a relevant context, then they will never truly grasp the concept.

Figure 16 – Mastery of a Concept

$$\begin{array}{r} \textit{Mechanics of Content} \\ + \ \textit{Meaning of Context} \\ \hline \textit{Mastery of a Concept} \end{array}$$

Content is driven by the absolute, whereas context has a strong relative component. The context of a task matters, provided it is relevant to the given learner. It is up to the teacher, therefore, to make a concerted effort to get to know the interests of his/her students and design tasks accordingly. Obviously no assigned task will be highly relevant to every student, but over the course of the year all students should have the opportunity to explore numerous tasks that are closely connected to their schema. What ultimately goes on the canvas represents the joy of teaching and the wonderment of learning.

Compound Interest

> ## *Inspire others to find their voice.*
> *Stephen Covey*

In the financial world, compound interest is generated when someone reinvests the initial interest he/she has earned. In layman's terms, it is all about earning interest on your interest. From a learner's lens, this surplus-driven motivator is the equivalent of getting increasingly committed to a task after having achieved initial success. As we all know, success breeds success. Since the task was rich and relevant to the learner, he/she is highly motivated to proceed with further exploration, and is driven to achieve even greater returns. This is the power of intellectual compound interest.

When students are given the freedom and encouragement to have real input into their areas of particular focus and real empowerment to pursue alternate paths to guide further explorations of a concept, their interest level just continues to rise. Then their intellectual inertia takes over, as they feed off their own ever growing passion for a given field of further study. In terms of establishing the framework for enjoying a rewarding life, acquiring an inherent interest in learning is more important than acquiring any specific facts or skills (Richardson, 2015).

Students develop an insatiable appetite for lifelong learning.

Another impactful yield from compound interest is inquiry learning. Inquiry is a student-centred search for deeper understanding that sparks the learner's natural sense of curiosity. The intellectual impetus behind these investigations is self-perpetuating, as new discoveries spawn more questions. The inquiry process is actually a microcosm of the Hour Glass metaphor, as students explore meaningful concepts that interest them, then apply their findings in new situations, which generates more queries and questions.

Within a risk-taking classroom culture based on invention and innovation, asking thought provoking questions, addressing misconceptions and mistakes triggered by inspired investigations, and proposing and defending theses are all more highly valued than simply getting the right answer. The students' existing schema is the starting point for inquiry-based learning, and then the teacher gradually releases responsibility as students gain more knowledge, skill, and confidence. Routine participation in inquiry learning develops critical thinking skills, raises student achievement, and improves students' attitudes towards learning (Hattie, 2009).

A powerful side benefit of having students routinely involved in pertinent inquiries is that their enthusiasm tends to rub off on classmates, who then also embrace these opportunities for new learning. A climate of confident and competent independent learning gradually permeates the entire classroom. Inquiry learning empowers students to ask, and attempt to answer, the questions about which they are most interested.

Inquiry learning leads to a change in the composition of each learner's schema backpack. Learners are learning from other learners and taking this information and assimilating it with existing beliefs based on their unique experiences. Not only is the composition of each schema backpack kept fluid from the constant influx of each student's own new experiences, but also from learning from others. Utilizing the contents of schema backpacks is also a great way to further involve students who typically struggle with academic work. They may well have unique experiences and expertise, and it does wonders for their enthusiasm and self-esteem to be regarded as the resident class experts on these topics.

Learners with a growth mindset generate by far the most compound interest, as in their eyes success is all about stretching themselves. It's about becoming smarter! Regardless of a given student's innate abilities, it is effort that turns these abilities into accomplishments, as the growth mindset promotes greater learning (Dweck, 2006).

The fixed mindset generates only simple interest, whereas the growth mindset generates compound interest.

R you routinely allowing students to apply this new learning with...

- **GENUINE PROBLEM SOLVING** *opportunities, rather than contrived demonstrations*
- **TRUE CREATIVE FREEDOM** *within* **ESTABLISHED PARAMETERS**
- *Routine opportunities to* **SHARE THEIR DISCOVERIES AND ENTHUSIASM WITH OTHERS**

The New 3 Rs Review

RICHNESS
R you routinely enriching tasks by…

- *Providing significant **DEPTH** and **BREADTH** to tasks, by transcending specific grade and subject*

- *Focusing on the **HOWS** and **WHYS** in all questioning and class discussions*

- *Emphasizing **COMPLEX TASKS** over Difficult Tasks*

RELEVANCE
R you routinely ensuring tasks are relevant to the learner by…

- *Acknowledging the **LEGITIMACY OF THE LEARNER'S LENS***

- *Providing the learner with **TIMELY AND RELEVANT FEEDBACK***

- *Triggering and maintaining **AUTHENTIC STUDENT ENGAGEMENT***

RETURN ON INVESTMENT
R you routinely providing students opportunities to apply this new learning with…

- ***GENUINE PROBLEM SOLVING** opportunities, rather than contrived demonstrations*

- *True **CREATIVE FREEDOM** within **ESTABLISHED PARAMETERS***

- *Opportunities to **SHARE THEIR DISCOVERIES AND ENTHUSIASM WITH OTHERS***

Reinvestment
The Inversion of the Hour Glass

Learning is the only thing the mind never exhausts, never fears and never regrets.
Leonardo Da Vinci

As much as the New 3 Rs of Teaching and Learning provide a powerful template for lifelong learning, there is an absolutely essential stage in this process that has yet to be addressed. The potential impact of learners generating a profitable return on investment based on rich, relevant tasks would be severely compromised without the all important 4th R: Reinvestment.

Traditional models of teaching and learning offer little opportunity for reinvestment, as each curriculum area receives its own distinct bird feeder, and at the end of the given unit of study the feeders are emptied to allow for future fillings. Each subsequent filling of each bird feeder is an isolated event that focuses on holding distinct data only until the next summative assessment.

Conversely, the Hour Glass model ensures, and requires, data to be cross-curricular as it is mixed together while generating rich tasks relevant to the given learner. While solving these problems, the learner acquires new skills that he/she then uses to explore future opportunities. The truest test to measure the legitimacy of any student's learning is the breadth and depth of its future applications while he/she confronts, and embraces, newly created rich, relevant tasks.

The ultimate goal of education is to teach our students *how to think*, not how to remember! Teachers must routinely model strategies for deeper thinking, and students will require regular practice developing these skills. Thinking skills transcend the confines of any specific curriculum, and will help our students approach new learning situations with both proficiency and passion.

Consequently, the initial filling of the lower chamber is far from the end of the learning cycle, as there will be several subsequent inversions of the Hour Glass. Each ensuing inversion signifies another reinvestment of new student learning.

As with financial enterprises, educational consumers derive dividends from the investment of time, energy, and expertise they have devoted to the exploration of the rich tasks. Reinvestment will be signified by the inverting, or flipping, of the Hour Glass after the vast majority of the learning from the original tasks has passed through. It is important to note that a portion of each task's input will remain in the filter until it becomes more relevant to the learner. Each reinvestment provides more opportunities for items remaining in the filter to become more relevant to the learner and adhere to the flow of subsequent rich tasks.

Each inversion of the Hour Glass signifies ongoing reinvestment in learning.

Prior to even pondering reinvestment, however, students need to have experienced numerous meaningful applications involving rich, relevant tasks. These applications then trigger new problems, passions, and potential pursuits. Reinvestment implies a heightened engagement by the learner into his/her future studies within the same general area of focus as directed by the original rich task. Students have now upped both their emotional and cognitive investment in the learning process, as with each reinvestment, or inversion of the Hour Glass, they are becoming increasingly committed to exploring these new, related tasks.

Each time the Hour Glass is inverted, the original Return On Investment domain now becomes the home of the new rich tasks. This inversion of the Hour Glass triggers a resynthesis, as these newly created rich tasks adhere to the learner's remaining relevant schema. Since these new questions and queries were cultivated from students applying new learning in authentic contexts, they already have a high degree of relevance to a given learner's schema and, therefore, a significant portion will swiftly funnel through the filter in the middle of the Hour Glass.

Figure 17 – Inverting The Hour Glass

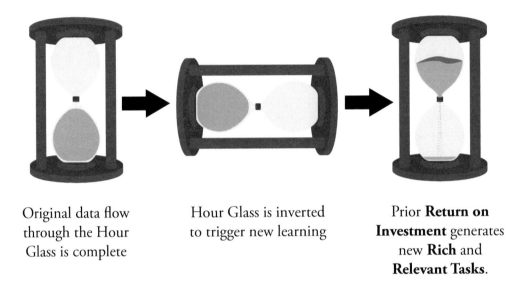

| Original data flow through the Hour Glass is complete | Hour Glass is inverted to trigger new learning | Prior **Return on Investment** generates new **Rich** and **Relevant Tasks**. |

With each subsequent inversion of the Hour Glass, less material will be trapped by the learner's filter, since a greater percentage of the input will already be in alignment with the individual learner's existing interests and experiences.

The Hour Glass inverts numerous times during a given unit of study.

Additional inversions of the Hour Glass will continue for the duration of the inquiries in which the student is engaged. There will be some residual material, not relevant to the learner, however, that will remain clogged in the filter indefinitely, and will never be used as the basis for future rich tasks and provide no return on investment. At the end of the inquiry, the Hour Glass is emptied and refilled, as brand new rich tasks will then trigger another series of inversions through the new 3 R process. The ongoing reinvestment of newly generated rich tasks is a critical component of meaningful learning and sustainable student interest in the material. Students learn more because they want to learn more! The challenge for the teacher is to ensure these rich tasks are embedded in the curriculum and that subsequent student explorations also stay within the realm of government expectations.

As Alvin Toffler stated, "The illiterate of the 21st century will not be those who cannot read and write, but those who cannot learn, unlearn, and relearn." It is the moral imperative of all educators to encourage and challenge a classroom full of inspired, independent learners. To help ensure that all learning opportunities are genuinely meaningful and motivating to all learners, assigned tasks must always address the new 3 Rs: **Richness, Relevance, and Return on Investment.**

The New 3 Rs vs The Traditional 3 Rs

Focus	Traditional 3 Rs	New 3 Rs
Metaphor	Bird Feeder	**Hour Glass**
Learning Indicators	Memorize Content	**Master Concept**
Learning Environment	Isolation	**Contextualization**
Learning In Action	Contrived Demonstration (Rote Following)	**Genuine Problem Solving (Route Forging)**
Learning Framework	High Floor – Low Ceiling	**Low Floor – High Ceiling**
Learner's Expectation	Fill Me Up	**Fulfill Me**
Learner Engagement	Behavioural Compliance	**Intellectual and Purposeful Connection**
Assessment Attitude	Knowing What To Show	**Yearning To Learn**
Assessment Tasks	Who? What? Where? When?	**How? Why?**
Assessment Priorities	Quantity	**Quality**
Assessment Process	Retrieval	**Application**

References

Blanchard, Ken. "How We Lead – Conversation On Leadership with Ken Blanchard." *Wordpress.* 7 January 2015. Web. 15 October 2016.

Briggs, Saga. "How To Make Learning Relevant To Your Students (And Why It's Crucial To Their Success)." *Inform ED. Open Colleges.* 4 October 2014. Web. 27 January 2017.

Capacity Building Series. *Student Identity and Engagement in Elementary Schools.* Service Ontario. May, 2011.

Covey, Stephen. *The 8th Habit – From Effectiveness to Greatness.* Simon & Schuster, 2013.

Dweck, Carol. *Mindset – The New Psychology of Success.* Random House Publishing, 2006.

Dweck, Carol. "Teachers' Mindsets – Every student has something to teach me." *Educational Horizons.* December 2014/January 2015.

Hattie, John. *Visible Learning: A Synthesis of Over 800 Meta-Analyses Relating to Achievement.* Routledge, 2009.

Hattie, John, Deb Masters and Kate Birch. *Visible Learning Into Action – International Case Studies of Impact.* Routledge, 2015.

Hargreaves, Andy and Dennis Shirley. *The Fourth Way: The Inspiring Future for Educational Change.* Corwin Publishing, 2009.

Heick, Terry. "6 Principles of Genius Hour in the Classroom." *Teachthought.* 28 September 2014. Web. 12 November 2016.

Katz, Steven and Lisa Ain Dack. *Intentional Interruption – Breaking Down Learning Barriers to Transform Professional Practice.* Corwin Publishing, 2013.

Klemm, William R. "Teaching Children To Think." *Psychology Today.* October, 2011.

Koo, Wai Mun. "The Invisible Lid." *PMO Bytes.* 17 July 2011. Web. 28 October 2016.

Morris, Tom. *The Art of Achievement: Mastering The 7 Cs of Success in Business and Life.* Andrew McMeel Publishing, 2002.

Olson, David R. and Steven Katz. 'The Fourth Folk Pedagogy'. *Understanding and Teaching the Intuitive Mind - Student and Teacher Learning.* Mahwah, NJ: Lawrence Erlbaum Associates, 2001.

Perkins, David. *Making Learning Whole – How Seven Principles of Teaching can Transform Education.* John Wiley & Sons, 2009.

Piggott, Jennifer. "Rich Tasks and Contexts." *NRICH. Millenium Mathematics Project.* February, 2011.

Quinn, Robert E., Katherine Heynoski, Mike Thomas, and Gretchen M. Spreitzer. *The Best Teacher in You: How to Accelerate Learning and Change Lives.* Berrett-Koehler Publishers, 2014.

Reeves, Douglas B. *Finding Your Leadership Focus – What Matters Most for Student Results.* Teachers College Press, 2011.

Richardson, Will. *Freedom To Learn.* Solution Tree Press, 2015.

Acknowledgements

Many thanks to all of the enthusiastic students, passionate educators, and supportive parents with whom I have had the pleasure and privilege of working throughout my career in public education.

Many thanks to my editorial team for adding numerous valuable insights and much appreciated encouragement at pivotal points throughout this journey.

Many thanks to Jordan and Ryan for all of your support, and, most of all, many thanks to Carol. Without your unwavering encouragement and very active support, this entire endeavour would not have been possible.